It's A Funny Old World

by
Carol A. Russell

authorHOUSE®

AuthorHouse™ UK Ltd.
500 Avebury Boulevard
Central Milton Keynes, MK9 2BE
www.authorhouse.co.uk
Phone: 08001974150

First published by AuthorHouse 3/26/2008

ISBN: 978-1-4343-7294-9 (e)
ISBN: 978-1-4343-7292-5 (sc)

Printed in the United States of America
Bloomington, Indiana

This book is printed on acid-free paper.

Dedication

To my friends and family who have been the source of much of my material!

Contents

It's A Funny Old World

It's a funny old world that we live in,
it's a funny old world, that's for sure,
with people as rich as Colossus
and those who are really dirt poor.

We all tread this earth and share footsteps
when we walk through this history as one,
we must sort out a main common language
and that's where the victories are won.

It's a world that we share with each other,
a world full of humour and fun,
as when you're living closely together
it's comedy wins friends one by one.

Fighting and battles and anger
never solve things, that's really a fact,
so let us make this agreement
to make the whole world join and laugh.

The world's getting closer together-
let's look on the bright side and joke.
As they say in the North, up in Yorkshire
There's nothing that's queerer than folk!

Traffic Lights

Popping up like mushrooms overnight
are the hated, road-works traffic lights.
They blink and make it clear
that no traffic's wanted here
and you wait, with motor running
'til green's bright.

And you motor and you crawl
and give the works an overhaul
and you see that there is no-one working there,
so you drive past even slower,
when generally you're a goer,
it's enough to make the mildest person swear!

Pop Star

Do you want to be a pop star
a star of stage and screen?
Do you want to be a pop star
the best that's ever been?

You'd sing and be on telly
you'd sing and crowds would scream,
you'd sing at music festivals
in wet and muddy fields

And when you're really famous
and known in everyplace-
you'd moan and say just leave me
I need quiet and my own space!.

Motor Racing

Driving round a race track isn't really fun.
Driving round the race track,
when you want to be number one.
When the tyres need constant changing
and the gears go all wrong,
driving round the racetrack isn't really fun

The mechanics blame the drivers
'cos they want to be number one
and the drivers blame mechanics
when they're not doing over a ton.
And the oil might need replacing
and the petrol mix is wrong,
driving round the racetrack in rain and in the sun

But when the motors humming
and your heartbeat picks up speed
you know that you're in racing
'cos it's the best life you could lead!

The Fatties Lament

I won't eat a bacon butty
I won't eat a chocolate bar
I won't eat that piece of cheesecake
or crisps shaped like a star

I won't eat a sausage sarnie
or chips that are nicely done
or eat jam roly poly
or a great big Chelsea Bun

I'll concentrate on salads
and seafood, fresh and good
I'll count all carbohydrates
on my plate of healthy food

I'll always drink pure water
no beer, spirits or wine
I'll sparkle through the morning
and in the afternoon I'll shine

I'll execise with fervour
I'll walk for miles and miles
I'll power-walk and weight- train
In this fight for longer time

I'll be the healthiest person
on our street, our neighbourhood
I'll be the perfect specimen
of healthy womanhood.

I'll live 'til way past 90
on this special fitness plan
I'll outlive friends and family
every woman, every man

And life will be so boring
I'll start eating once again
and live just 'til I'm 80
on my moderate, careful plan.

But maybe it's just better
to have some fun instead
and live until I'm 75
and die fat and drunk in bed!!!!!

DIY

With hammer and chisel
some nails and some screws
I want to create something
something quite new.

With brushes and varnish
sandpaper and saw
I'll create something useful
to stand on the floor

Now should it be wardrobes
or bookshelves
or chest?
The question is really
what could I do best?

Some paper, a ruler
a pencil and pen
I'll mock up some drawings,
some vision
and then

I'll knock it together
 with consummate ease
a masterpiece, no doubt-
a Vision to please.

I'll just make a coffee,
a sandwich and then
I will get to the matter
with a stroke of the pen

And while in the kitchen
I'll make something good
some supper for everyone,
nutritious hot food

The time's running out
for my master-piece,
my DIY special,
I'll do it next week.
Maybe IKEA has a flat pack instead
I'll review that tomorrow-
but now, time for bed!

Thinking on a Star

Twinkle, twinkle little star
can you see me from afar,
watching every move I make
when I sleep and when I wake?

Twinkle twinkle little star
I'd like to put you in a jar
and look at you shining there
and no-one else will be aware

of all that brightness
all that power
as you shine for us
each and every hour.

Star that's shining extra bright
are you just a satellite
watching all of us at play
every night and every day?

Watching when we're home at rest
or even when we're at our best.
Do you know the things we do?
You see lives clearly, through and through

Who is it that wants to know
all our details, head to toe.
Watch out if they're feeling smug
as someone just might pull the plug!

Talk

We used to talk to one another.
We used to talk face-to-face.
We used to talk to one another
in the same room, in the same place.

But now we 'phone each other,
we text or send e-mail.
we 'facebook', blog and skype each other,
but never meet face to face

And while we fail to face each other,
and while we see no smile,
we build a gap between us
which widens mile by mile.

But when we see each other
having travelled many miles,
we'll see the face of friendship
and we'll recognise the smiles

And peace will gain a friend then
when men meet eye to eye
and they'll try to understand then,
and reduce technology files.

The Heron

We bought a plastic heron
to sit out by our pond
to guard our lovely goldfish
of which we're very fond

You see, a real-life heron
had been eating up our fish,
his daily luncheon menu-
they were his favourite dish.

The theory is with herons
they do not know the score
and if there's one already
they won't come knocking at the door

The life-like plastic Heron
would make the real-one think
there's a heron there already
I'll find some other place to drink.

Now the heron in our garden
must be a special one
as when he saw the model,
he thought 'I will have some fun'

I'm lonely when I come here
I'd like to have a mate
this one doesn't seem to talk much
I hope I'm not too late

So on a daily basis
our herons, side by side,
make a picture of perfect friendship
a fact we cannot hide

They come up close together
like old friends from afar
and as they've made such friendship
I think I'll start a spa.

So come on all you Herons
come from miles and miles
and I'll hand out your welcome drinks
clear water- heron style!

Colds and Things

No-one uses handkerchiefs to stop those coughs and sneezes,
people seem to use their coats and cardigans and sleavses.
So now we need a rethink, before this goes much further,
so let us look at where we're at, consider it with fervour.

Behaviour of our legends affects our patterns too,
and sometimes looking at their ways, they should live in
a zoo!
When sportsmen run across a grassy wide and muddy field
they spit and cough out on their mates, no matter what
the teams.

The sportsmen with a cold, it seems is not a man to know,
even though he toughs it out in hail or wind or snow.
If he has to wipe his nose when running in a game
he'll cast his germs towards the wind without a touch of
shame.

The trouble doesn't stop at that you really must beware,
as coughs and colds and nasty things are breeding everywhere.
And when you're shopping in the street and chatting
with your neighbours
you must really watch out for the flu, so do yourself a favour.

Tell your friends and teach your kids, a simple thing in
manners-
'Wipe Your Nose with a Handkerchief'- should we put it
on a banner?
To get this message out to all, to **all** across the country
Keep Your Germs Just To Yourself-it's really ELIMENTARY!

Leaving School

No-one really likes school,
we all know that for sure
as when it gets to end of term
they're rushing out' the door

No more special projects.
No more sums in maths.
No more putting our results
in the form of graphs.

No more crass school dinners.
No more early morns.
No more writing homework
or filling in the forms

No more noisy classrooms,
or noisy corridors.
No more class assemblies
or lining by the doors.

And when we meet outside school,
we all can breathe again
Am I talking of the pupils?
No, it's teachers and their friends!

The Tax Man Cometh

And so we come to that time of year
when we move on from Christmas cheer.
The letter's dropped down on the mat
and we remember the time that
we must declare just what we earn
and fill in our own tax return

The letter says in red inch high
that if you're late you get a fine.
And so it is with trembling pen
I start to write, then start again.
I must declare all to be taxed,
I do not want to make him vexed

So now I groan and make a sigh
I chew my pen and blink my eyes,
then bite the bullet, here I go
nice and steady, nice and slow.
Well what do you know I am not late
And they owe me a tax rebate!

Who are You?

What facet do you see today?
What facet of my life.
Do you see a daughter, sister, mother, colleague,
cousin, auntie, wife.

Each woman holds Pandora's box
of characters of kin,
and layer on layer you seek to find
what's in the depths within.

The outside shell, the one the world
sees on a regular basis
is only <u>one</u> that's recognised
of many of the faces.

The cared-for and the caring,
the one, supporting needs
of the vulnerable, the weary
helping others to succeed.

Provider of contentment,
the laughter and the love.
The one who others seek to find
to walk with hand in glove.

The protector and protected,
the lover and the friend,
complications of the complex
the messages you send.

Solitaire

When I find I've time to spare
I pass it playing solitaire.
Not the one with proper cards
but the other one that's not so hard

The one that has 'n 'lectronic face,
the one that's based on cyberspace.
The cards move places by a mouse
-not the one that scurries around the house

You find contentment when you've done
you've played the game and find you've won,
the music sings and fireworks blaze.
You've scored these points, the message says

But then you see the counter's score
and see it's greater than before,
so you've not won at all, you say,
it's worse than when I played yesterday.

I'll have another go and see
if I can beat the best of me.
The really bad computer-man
hears your wish and plans a plan.

The next ten games you try to play
are worse by far than yesterday.
Not only yesterday, you find
but every game you had in mind.

So in the end you give right in-
and think you'll go and pour a gin.
But then you score the best score yet,
he's got you hooked, try another set.

The time goes on and on and on,
I'll stop this game, it won't take long.
The clock continues – now midnight
and you just look a dreadful sight

Like Cinderella at the ball
you must leave, or lose it all.
And so you drag yourself away,
but save the game for another day!

Christmas

Christmas is coming
the geese are getting fat,
and you'll be getting fatter
there's no question about that

With Christmas Eve
drinks parties,
and friends around to greet,
you're bound to have some nibbles
while standing on your feet

And then there's Christmas dinner,
a treat for everyone,
with mounds of Christmas turkey,
and Christmas pudding
steeped in rum

And then there's after Christmas
eating up those turkey bits,
and sandwiches and curries
and sausages on sticks.

And then you face the weigh scales
and see those mounting pounds
and mark that magic moment
when you make a howling sound

I can't have put much weight on!
It wasn't that much food!
I had to let my hair down!
I had to share the mood!

But, there's New Year coming next week
with resolutions for all men
I'll start my fitness programme
and diet once again!

Sales

Have you ever been to one of those
'After-Christmas Sales',
where assistants all look harassed
and the managers look pale

Where multitudes of shoppers
come dashing through the door
to buy that special bargain
that they had missed before

Where pyramids of wonders
cascade to form a treat
and you can't find a sitting place
to rest your weary feet

And miles and miles of shoppers
have made another queue
to form a barricade five deep
just right in front of you

There's bargains here for everyone.
There's presents to be bought.
There's slippers, shirts and cardigans.
There's tons of stuff to sort.

There's talc for Aunty Margaret,
there's golf balls for her son,
there's pens and socks for your old dad
and then you're nearly done.

The wrapping paper's next to find,
it really is a treat
I'll take five rolls before it's gone,
it won't be here next week.

The list goes on for pages
I'll really have to find
a little gift for everyone,
that's what I've got in mind.

I know it's only one day
since we had our turkey cheer
but, the sale is our treat for Boxing Day
to provide our gifts for next year.

Box of Buttons

Do you have a box full of buttons,
buttons of all shapes and size,
for cardigans, coats, shirts and trousers
and even for teddy bear's eyes?

There's a story behind every button,
a story not usually told.
There are buttons quite new and exciting
and some that are just very old.

There's the one that is white from your school shirt,
the one from the neck where it meets
but you recall you never sewed it,
your tie covered the gap underneath.

There's the black one from grandad's old waistcoat,
it came off and it went down the chair,
so he never bothered to button it
and displayed all his underwear!

The shiny and sparkly white button
came from a blouse you once bought
for a shiny and bright Christmas party,
where you looked 'really great', so you thought!

There's the one from the baby's first jacket,
the one that grandmother knit,
it's a yellow and smiley cute duckling
and you picture the chair where she'd sit.

The box full of buttons tells a story,
a story since your life began
and the pictures it brings to your memory
are better than any album

So next when you're needing a button
go and look in your special box,
be amazed at the selection before you
and listen, as each of them talks!

Right Royal Mail

In hail and wind and sun and snow
just watch our little postie go
delivering letters for you and me
before he gets home for his tea.

A bill for water, a bill for gas
electric bill and then at last,
there is a postcard from a friend,
I'll leave that 'till the very end

I've won a prize, the letter reads,
just 'phone this number there's no need
to get yourself into a frenzy-
the voice on the line is never ending.

But what's this here? I'd like to know,
he's brought me this through hail and snow
a special gift, a new appeal
will I leave my earnings in a Will?

Why can't we just have letters from
our sister, uncle, auntie, mum,
every mailing seems to bring
a pile of rubbish, ah, but still

It's good to see our postman friend
who carries on to the bitter end,
and while we're tucked up warm in bed
he's sorting out our post, instead.

Snowtime

Do you remember years ago
when you used to play out in the snow?
You'd run and slide and fall about,
you'd scream and laugh and smile and shout.

You'd slide down on your special sledge
 when racing -try to get the edge
over other kids sliding down the hill
showing off their steering skill.

Snowballs flying through the air
in all directions everywhere.
You'd try to hit a moving goal
and miss- but hit another soul

And then the snowman not too stable
the next job on your snow timetable.
Roll the head round on the ground,
make it strong and firm and round

Try to make the body then
it doesn't look like any men
that I see wandering round the street
'cos he just don't have any feet!

Then back you'd go with mum and dad,
what a special time you'd had
with freezing hands and freezing feet,
still it was a special treat.

But now the snow has disappeared,
the climate change is to be feared.
Will our own grandchildren ever
have such fun, or wild endeavours?

The politicians tell us all-
halt climate change, however small.
How many listen to that request?
How many people do their best?

Whatever happens we all know
the future of earth's ice and snow
won't be our problem, we'll have gone,
but winter?- maybe there'll be none.

You Gotta Have A Lotta Bottle

The species 'British Milkman'
Is a rare and dying breed
Bringing milk right to your doorstep
And other things that you need.

He brings along your pinta
In the morning for your tea
He takes away the empties
For recycling, you see

There's bread and eggs and bacon
He brings round on his van
And cream and cheese and veggies
And yoghurt, even lamb.

He's a very special species
That we must all support
Or else the supermarket
Will be our only thought
When we go to buy our 'full fat'
Our 'light' or semi- skimmed
The choice'll be 'take or leave it'
The rest will have been binned

Our species 'British Milkman'
Is needed, without doubt
They give a special service
That's British all throughout.

It's the personal touch of service
It's the smile that greats the dawn
It's the watchful eye on safety
On our vulnerable every morn.

So support your very own milkman
Give him your order now
For your weekly regular order
And for extras, make a vow

You won't rush off to Tesco
To Asda, Waitrose too
Or Sainsbury or Budgeon's
Just take this point of view

I want you Mr Milkman
Not to disappear
So 'Get Lost' supermarket
And give the milkman a great big cheer!!!

Onions

Peeling onions makes you cry,
it makes you sigh and wipe your eye
and then the tears begin to flow
and you can't see now where to go

And then you try to wipe them dry
and smear your finger as you try.
Your eyes now stream- now what to do
so you can have a clearer view?

You stumble to the kitchen sink
and wash your hands, then have a drink,
while seeing all through smarting eyes
you begin now to philosophise.

Perhaps I'll cook with frozen foods
or even dried stuff, that's quite good.
I must not make mistakes again
while chopping onions, that's quite plain

But what the heck the food is good-
next time I'll just wear a hood!

Ambitions

I'd like to be a conductor,
a conductor of a band
or a leader of an orchestra
with a baton in my hand.

I'd wave my hands in earnest
and look quite serious too
and keep all the wind section
especially in view

We'd play for special people
who really did respect
the hours and hours of practice
and the commitments that we'd kept.

We'd specialize in Mozart,
in Beethoven and in Bach,
we'd dabble in Shostakovich
and play Haydn in the park.

We'd play from eve 'til morning
and then we'd start again,
we'd play from morn 'til eve-time
from dawn 'til half past ten.

We'd be a special team then
that all the world would want,
we'd play for Royal patrons
and in fancy restaurants.

Until the offer comes through
I'll practice on my own
in front of the bedroom mirror
with a biro in my hand

I'll dream the special players
are there in front of me,
and when we've finished playing,
they can all pop round for tea!

I'll dream about the audience,
the TV and the crew,
the cameramen and reporters
will have to join the queue

But who is it I'm kidding?
I'll never have that chance.
So maybe one day, just instead
perhaps I'll learn to dance!

Angel Baker

Who would be a baker
working through the night,
with flour and eggs and all those things
for baking things just right?

With cakes and scones to bake yet,
there's half a ton of flour
and sugar, jam and honey
being used up by the hour.

There's carrot cake and flapjack
and banoffee, best of all,
there's meringue and cake with chocolate in,
you can really have a ball

There's croissants for your breakfast
and teacakes for your tea.
There's cheesecake, dates and currant buns
all for you and me

And when you next go shopping
and buy your loaf of bread,
remember the dear old baker
at work while you're in bed!

And smile next when you great him,
give him a cheery grin
sing a song that says 'good morning',
the world's better here with him.

We need you Mr Baker
so keep baking every day
and we'll keep saying 'Thank you'
each in our own special way!

The Christmas Tree

In rich and fertile ground
the Christmas Tree stands proud,
fed by earth beneath it
and watered by the clouds

By day with light and sunshine,
at night bright, starry skies,
reaching ever upwards
with its strength, its shape, its size.

The growing year continues
until December, when
The Christmas Tree is looked at
by many different men.

Its height, its weight its branches
are regulated so
it will be the choice of shoppers
and all the folks they know.

So the Christmas tree is severed
from the roots that hold it firm,
then to a car it's tethered
and the journey is confirmed

To go to its destination
to be hung with dressings there,
to bring along great pleasure
with other festive fayre

The tinsel and the baubles
are all brought out again,
it is spangled and then bangled
and the fairy lights brought in.

And when it gets to Twelfth Night
all decorations go
into the loft of houses
for the next twelve months or so.

And the proud and splendid fir tree
gets put out on the ground
to be dumped along with others
when the dustbin men call round.

I'm sorry little fir tree
that we treat you with such shame,
so next year I'll buy artificial
and stop this destruction game!

Christmas Alone

In a quiet room on Christmas night,
the woman sits alone,
sipping sherry,
watching Tv,
remembering the memories
of Christmases come and gone.
The cat purrs quietly at her feet.
The quiet street and closed doors
echo in their
abandonment.
She raises her glass and smiles a cheery
'Here's to you, puss'.
There is no stirring from the sleeping cat,
but still she drinks her festive glass
then raises it again and ruefully says:
'And Here's to Me
Good Health, Good Cheer.
And Here's to Me for a Happy New Year'

Age

When you are over fifty
you're deemed thirty now, we're told
time now for new adventures
try new things and be bold.

So go and try out new things
horse riding, skiing, art
hill -walking, swimming, singing
so much, now, where to start?

Now life is split to seasons
and this is the summer time
So now, before the autumn,
get active -get in line.

Oh yes, you're over fifty
When life begins again
You can read the book you meant to
Read one?, no, make it ten.

You can buy a pair of glasses,
the trendy ones of course,
and make it look as though you're
part of the intellectual force.

The dentist may need a visit,
you can book it right away,
as now you're a private patient
you can always have your say

Your smile will look just perfect,
bright shiny, and quite white,
with nashers like a young'un
stars will hide away at night.

So what! you're over fifty,
you'll wow the crowds again,
on the dance floor and the catwalk
you'll proudly strut and then

you'll step towards the Autumn,
the Autumn of your years
and when it gets to Winter
you won't have regretful tears!

Travel

So you're on your way to the airport
to go and have some fun
all packed up and you're ready
for your holiday in the sun

But then you look before you
at the long security queue
as there are now a hundred souls
just right in front of you

You shuffle meekly forward
with your bag all neatly arranged
or should you have brought two bags
the regulations may have changed

You dare not raise a smile now
at the person checking you through
as a chat or a quip or even a grin
mean they might detain you.

They might think that you've gone barmy
or had a drink or two,
you might upset the passengers
who journey on with you

But now you're through the checking,
you're really on your way
and you look up to the screens above-
your plane has a three hour delay!

The British Countryside

Walking through the countryside
is a sign of British life
Walking through the countryside
a man, dog, children, wife.

The walks in British countryside
really are a dream
with lovely British wildlife,
in the fields and woods and streams.

And as you take your walk now
along the farmer's meadow
you might see sheep and cows there
or horses and their shadows.

Now marching through the country
you notice that you put
your foot down on some debris
in the walkway underfoot

It does not really matter,
you mutter to yourself
as you've put on your walking boots
which were resting on the shelf.

Oh look, there is a robin,
a swan, a falcon too,
Does anyone remember
How far is the nearest loo?.

Now concentrate your mind now
look round at what there is
to keep your thoughts on nature
and not where you'd like to sit.

Ah, there's another treasure
of our British countryside
the squirrel busy finding nuts
and other things to hide.

And walking boldly onwards
you find another view
of paper, butts and sandwich wraps
MacDonalds is there too.

You're finishing your walk now
and really feeling great
you'll walk again quite soon now
before it is too late
as the route you have just taken
won't be there by next year,
for they're building two hundred houses
with supermarket too quite near.

Strictly Dancing

When I heard of Strictly
on BBC TV,
I thought 'It's not a programme
of any interest to me.'

I remember learning Ballroom
on a Saturday afternoon,
with golden shoes and flairy skirts
and old fashioned music tunes.

We'd dance in a hall together
round the room, a bit like a herd
and try to smile, and point our toes
in second, first and third.

We'd chasis, glide and cha cha
and turn and glide again,
then all go home and watch TV
and say goodbye to our friends.

I sometimes watched 'Come Dancing'
at home with dad and mum
where dancers glided round the floor
in competition.!

I never thought that Strictly
would take off like a dream,
where households every Saturday night
were glued to every screen.

We've all got hooked on lycra,
on sequins, boas too,
the blokes look good in white tie
with their hair stuck down like glue.

Our love goes to the dancers
who work and train all week
to hone their skills and stances,
they need a competitive streak.

We watch our football legends
and actors from the soaps
get involved in dancing
and raise our respective hopes,
that all our favourite heroes
will get through to next week,
with Samba, Jive and Foxtrot
and the Waltz, a special treat.

With judges there to make them
feel their effort's really weak,
you'd think the stars would bolt away,
 but they stand there looking meek.

They take the comments boldly
and squarely on the chin,
they lose a stone 'bout every week
by the fourth week- they're looking thin!

We're really hooked on Strictly
we do not miss a show,
we watch it every Saturday
and each weekday night, you know.

The members of the panel
are like our family now,
it's like each home at Christmas
when everyone has a row!

The crystal ball as trophy
is a reminder to the team
that they must raise their standards
to make the final scene.

And when the final's over
and the dancing all is done,
we'll go back to boring programmes
about holidays in the sun!!

The Issue

And he stood there
resolute,
knowing that
at the sound of his voice
the passing parade of
commuters and
office workers
would march more boldly
towards their destination

'Big Issue'?,
he would say.
And their heads would go down
with their eyes averted
to find another spot
to gaze.

'Big Issue'?,
he repeats
to deafened ears
and silent souls
who do not wish to
recognise his presence.

An elderly woman,
a single soul
in the passing crowd,
reaches to her purse
to proffer the coffers
of hope
to this abandoned soul.

A gesture from the needy
to the needy,
avoiding the greedy
thoughts of the
marching army
hiding their heads
beneath their mantle
of self determination

New Land

They came in their thousands
to start a New World.
They came in their thousands
not knowing a word
of the language their masters would utter in vain.
Where the sights and the sounds would not be the same
as the home and the friendships that they left behind,
when they started their journey to this new Promised Land.
United in difference
they'd all take a stand

Where no recognition of sights and new sounds
would surround them and drown them
in their new parent land.
Where the humble, the pious, the rough and the meek
would step out together,
live in the same street.
The smells of the cooking,
the sounds of the voice
would all come together
in the land of their choice

What sights left behind them?
What cries did they hear?
What pictures of hardship
in their memories seared?
What hopes for the future?
What secrets in mind,
of knowing the hardships
of those left behind.?

Healthy Living

In the centre of your life's detritus,
is the cause of your general arthritis.
Too much meat, too much wine,
too much having a good time,
So eat wise-what a bore day and night is!

The Royal Bird

In our garden there is a male pheasant,
whose life is remarkably pleasant,
with three females in tow
he is quite a beau,
and he feels like a king not a peasant!

Doctor's Waiting

Have you recently been to see
your friendly neighbourhood GP,
for a cold or the flu
or something quite new
or even a twinge in your knee

Where you wait several minutes in line
for your doctor's appointment time
for your own special friend
you'll be seen at the end
of the surgery- now sure you don't mind?

Now you could just have telephoned in,
not to do so is really a sin,
but you reasoned that you
would be better in view
and they really might 'just fit you in'

The receptionist's unfriendly stare
makes you wish you were not standing there,
as they're busy, you know,
and you wish that they would show
just a smile or a signal of care.

If you'd booked by email when online
you'd be sure of an appointment time,
but the computer's so cold
and you're feeling so old
to your waiting you just 'come resigned!

50

So it's two hours or more now before
you came through the surgery door
and you're now feeling better
you'll just send a letter
you'll be needing their service no more!

But just then, in time, comes a shout-
is it your name that they are calling out?
We're sorry for waiting
and without hesitating
your prescriptions in your hand and you're out!!!

The Vacuum

The vacuum's a wond'rous invention
and one now we mostly don't mention,
as we skim like a breeze
through our housework with ease
which these days hardly causes us tension!

Our forebears through moaning and groaning,
would have knelt on the floorboards and stoning,
they'd scrub and they'd rub,
and they'd push and they'd shove
to clear bugs and dustmites 'til morning!

Sellotape

Sellotape on reels can be a problem.
You think you've get it sorted, oh but damn them.
They tear and then they tangle
and you really cannot handle
that your parcel seems it's wrapped up by a vandal!

The Stapler

The creature in everyone's office
needs care- tell your office novice.
On chocolate do not try it
and fudge'll cause a riot,
as a stapler's jaws just need a staple diet!

The Ruler

The ruler's a wonderful treasure
if there is something you want to measure.
If you measure by inch
it thinks it's a cinch,
but by metric it's life is a pleasure!

Gutters

Nobody talks about gutters.
Not a single word is ever uttered.
But without them you see,
we would sink to our knees
'neath the rain and the debris that splutters!

Getting the Right Angle

A protractor or a compass
must be in every set
for the mathematics student
to become the teacher's per

You can measure every angle.
You can draw a circle round.
You can calculate degrees
and other students you confound.

And when you sit there smugly
with all your answers done,
you say to all your friend's there
'Need any help, my son?'

And then the students gather
round about you and then vent,
their total group resentment
and you wish you never sent
for that mathematics class set
the best one from the store
and you throw it in the waste bin
'nd swear you'll use it never more!

The Dentist

Waiting for the dentist
in the waiting room
you know that you will see him
very,very, soon.

Waiting for the dentist
you read a magazine
and see the models on the page
with smiles that are serene.

Waiting for the dentist
it won't be very long.
Before your turn just comes around
you'll hum a happy song

You'll hum about the good times
as through life you me-andered
then think about those woesome days
when out of line you wandered.

You should have paid attention to those
bright and pearly whites
if you're to keep them in your mouth
not in a tooth- glass at night.

The chocolates and the sweeties
the sugar and the rest
you should have left them all alone
for your teeth to be their best

Here comes the dentist's nurse now
It's time to take the chair.
Now think of where you'd like to be
if you weren't just sitting there.

Your mouth is opened widely
and prodded and then polished
and rinsed and sparkled through now-
and you've not been admonished!

So off you tread toward home now,
it's wonderful to be
free of the pain and misery
in other patients that you see.

So goodbye Mr Dentist,
we'll meet again next year,
and I will rest for months again,
before I face the fear!

Fatherhood

And so you've come to fatherhood
and doing things a parent should,
like making feeds and changing nappies
all to make your new son happy.

And then a voice speaks in your head
and says the things <u>your</u> father said
'bout what to say and what to do
to help your babe and your wife too

The sleepless nights and early feeds
to answer all your baby's needs,
will keep you busy, in the house
and at the shops, there is no doubt.

But this young man is so worth while
he'll make you laugh and make you cry,
he'll make you proud and make you sigh,
he'll put a sparkle in your eye.

He'll crawl and walk and then he'll run,
he'll give you both a life of fun.
He'll swim, he'll read, he'll sing, he'll smile
he'll make you run mile after mile

At school and clubs your son will shine,
he'll be the apple of your eye.
He'll grow up tall and smart and then
no longer child he'll join the men

And as he grows with seamless ease
he'll start upon a football field
and choose a team of great renown,
you've guessed, of course, it's Harlow Town!

About the Author

Carol A. Russell was born and educated in Leeds. In 1968 she left Leeds to go to Whitelands College, London, to study Drama and Education, graduating with B. Ed in 1972. She taught in London and on The Isle of Sheppey, Kent, before moving to Sawbridgeworth in Hertfordshire in 1975. For the next 30 years, she taught in schools and community groups in both Essex and Hertfordshire and was the founder in 1987, of Youth CREATE, a Community Arts organisation, which she ran until her retirement in 2006. She has written numerous lyrics, songs and plays with music. This is her first publication of poetry. She continues to live in Sawbridgeworth with her husband and family.

Printed in the United Kingdom
by Lightning Source UK Ltd.
128540UK00001B/46-51/P